Where God Learns

In loving gratitude for these true teachers—
Ruth Davids, 1909-1986
Ellen Potter Hall, 1898-
Raymond Tyner, 1924-1988
Vernon Harry, 1911-2001

Where God Learns

Rusty C. Moe

Black Moss Press
2002

Published by Black Moss Press at 2450 Byng Road, Windsor, Ontario N8W 3E8, Canada. Black Moss books are distributed in Canada and the U.S. by Firefly Books. All orders should be directed there.

"Merton's Woods" © Mark Van Doren. Reprinted by permission from the executors of the estate of Mark Van Doren.

Cover photograph courtesy of Vernon Harry and Jerrilyn Jackson Moe.

Author photograph by Lloyd Brooks.

Design by Karen Veryle Monck.

ISBN 0-88753-376-0

☙ TABLE OF CONTENTS

Part One

Part Two

... inside human beings is where God learns
–Rainier Maria Rilke
(translation by Robert Bly)

Part One

≈ Whispering Hope—A Magnificat

*For what does one have to atone most? For one's
modesty: for having failed to listen to one's
most personal requirements; for having mistaken oneself;
for having underestimated oneself;
for having lost a good ear for one's instincts;
This lack of reverence for oneself revenges itself
through every kind of deprivation: diminishing
one's health, friendship, well-being, pride,
cheerfulness, freedom, firmness, and courage*
–Frederich Nietzsche

Creation and its liberation,
earth and its heaven, swell
in my lifeblood,
and I dwell
in the praise
of this great vow.
I contain the seed of the Most High,
have been chosen—as has everyone—
as wet-nurse to the Infinite.
I have been anointed by God's breath—
blessed be those wise lungs!

The Divine Rose grows
within the heart
of each generation,
protecting and shepherding
those who waken
to Its fire and Its scent—
all others drown
in the tepid riddles
of their own time.

The strong shall grieve;
the helpless shall dance.
The famished will be filled
and the wealthy ravaged
by their own appetites.

We magnify You,
Ancient-And-Ever-Newborn:
You have heard us,
and You have borne us
out of our darkness
and into the clear light
of Your Merciful Secret.

❧ The Flesh Recalls Itself In Silence

The flesh recalls itself in silence.
All this dust, soothed,
loosens its clasp
'round the sighing soul,
tunes the heart
to a lower pitch,
receives the sole tone,
anechoic and slow,
within an oval chamber:
pinkish, hushed, alert.

We have been burned into being
out of creation's need for itself,
hewn out of a ceaseless desire
that seeks its own, undying forms.
Without thought
and with total purpose,
a great Word,
a lone urge
seethes beyond the fiction of the face.

∾ Lovers in the Sleeping Nerve

Nowhere else are the original mystery
and the outward reality so near
to each other as in love.
                    –Max Picard

The birds are at their genius—
reinventing dawn.
Beneath our mosque
of pillow and quilt,
we rouse *adagio,* swelled and oiled
by sleep's largesse,
turn to *Yes*
as easily as streams
dream of water.

There is no dressage:
pumpkins grow without epic
or urgency.
We love because we can
(and for the love of love)—
turn hair to hymns
with *a tempo* hands,
mouths' mucous
to Cana's triumph.

And the collapse to Eden
is pale destination
beside the burgeoning map
of our hot trust.

≋ *Semen Christianorum* – St. John's Hymn

The Unbegun begins to waken within a faithful few.
One of these slowly comes to, realizes how his true nature has always
been (will always be) one with the Spirit of the earth of paradise;
that all things, animate or not, are created within, and through, this
Bounteous Spirit.
Here is a true life that can lighten the life of anyone,
a seemly life, gleaming amidst ignorance—but ignored, despite its
wild glory.
Another man, a man named John, notices the Balefire showing Itself
through his kinsman
and begins to witness to this Opener of the Way: "Let those who are
still enough and those who see with the Eye of their eyes or hear
with the Ear of their ears be rent by perfect love."
But fear is our numbing custom, and to only a few is the Opener not
a fire-hearted fool.
But those who rise up and walk into the arms of tender liberation
and tenderer mercy,
are re-created—not by ideas, genetics, or justice—but by the Herb of
Grace and Truth:
spermata tou logou is growing a taproot among us while we sigh and
revel shyly in the presence of the Human Being, fully (and finally)
revealed.

≈ Your Hand Has Become a Cliché

Your hand has become a cliché—
curves, curls, creases, contours,
hieroglyphic veins,
knuckleskin of wrinkled flowerets,
thready map of pilgrim hair.

I surrender to it as I do
to any weather that freezes hay
in lofts, renders branches
suave beneath peasant snows,
ages honey and malt to mead;
meet it as wing meets air,
trusting the drafts and thrusts
of current.

Your hand furls my tensile flesh
like birches' bark;
nerve and color
rend and re-invent me.

∾ *Tehillim* (Praise Songs)

for Pastor Steve Moore and Fr. Gabriel Baltes, O.S.B.

...the Psalms have been used as the Jewish hymnal since several centuries B.C. and by Christendom since Apostolic times...praising God for God's existence, they did not have to undertake the search, which today is so much a matter of desperation...there is no book anywhere in the world which implies that the existence of the thing believed in does not depend upon the belief itself...any praise would be understatement...the ardor of the psalmist never cools...though he is limited in theme, he seems to recognize no limit among the images and epithets which a burning imagination may command...the original number can never be known...a re-filtering, a distillation [of] a particular language which has now become the model of what great English speech can be...the quality of music in them is resonance matched with reason....

**–Irwin Edman, Louis Untermeyer, and
Mark Van Doren in conversation, 1941**

∾ Praise Song 23

I am cared for, tended to,
and freely adored
by God, Who made me
for stillness and wonder.
Abundance is my birthright.
Even when I tremble in the throes
of heartbreak and darkening wounds,
I can trust,
for I am always protected and fed,
my fevers are always cooled.
Bells of joy peel me open!
As long as I live (and even after),
I will walk in Healing Beauty.

≈ Praise Song 137

Our peasant remnant collapsed beneath the willows near the acid
bogs of Babylon, mourning our Mother, Jerusalem.
We hid our music in the silent, silver limbs,
for our kidnappers heckled us, saying, "Laugh now, you orphaned
Semites! Now sing of your Great Mother's majesty and might!"
Frolic and sing? How could we? Without our own land, we are
voiceless.
Tender Mother, strike me dumb, if I forget that you are my spirit's
womb;
melt my tongue if my eyes ever leave the angels of Your presence.
Remember the descendants of Esau, Mother—garroters who meas-
ured Your destruction with plumb-lines. "Raze her!" they shouted.
"Raze her to her footings and salt her!"
O, Babylon, about to be aborted: blessed is She Who butchers you!
Blessed is She Who cleaves the darling dove-skulls of your heinous
infants!

≈ Praise Song 8

Amma, we sing Your holy name with our whole hearts.
Your beauty and Your bounty flood the cosmos.
Infants and sucklings adore You perfectly; their total trust shames
every evil wind.
Awed, my Lady, by the intricacies of earth and sky, we dare to ask:
"Who—what—are we that You care enough to dwell among us?"
You have made us of dark clay—not angel-stuff—and yet, You crown
us with the myrtle of awareness and clothe us in robes of finest sensa-
tion. You have entrusted us with the discovery and the naming and
the ordering of Your creation.
Mother of our years, with our genius and our wantonness we praise
You.

≋ Praise Song 121

I raise my eyes
to Jehovah-shammah,
Who always provides.
My health comes
from the Mountain of Salvation.
My footing is sure and assured:
the One who formed me is all eye;
the One who formed
the Islands of the Blessed is all verb;
the One who formed you
sees Itself through you.
Do not be seduced
by hot judgments
nor succumb to the coils
of false music.
Your soul shall be faithfully shielded
and made radiantly muscular
by Jehovah-shammah;
the rhythms of your golden breath
shall be counted
until everything is possible.

≈ Barnlight

Gambrel-roofed and red as reaper rust,
facing west alone, the barn
could be a minor prophet's face
or the face of a cliff at Moher.
See the wheat around it growing old
in the ageing heat and growing gold.
Smell the wells and watered earth,
the sweetening yarrow and goldenrod.

There is no music,
despite the sun's Gregorian slant;
this heaving hymn has no mouth,
though shadows yearn with a cello's tongue.
This small, unspired silence
is a cleft in the patience of the Lamb.
Come, trust: trust is every breath
(or the wet breath on a mirror).
The light has cleaved itself
into yellow and glory,
and every face you ever loved
who knew and never doubted you is here,
indivisible from history or hope.

The white-pine sides were painted
(in a once beyond local memory),
with a powdered ochre-and-buttermilk batter—
brushed on, brushed in, brushed out—
with brushes made of basswood bark
soaked in lye and beaten—
so the lapping light

broods without burdening,
girds without wearying.
Come inside:
be pressed and released,
pressed and released,
by a quiet cascade of civilized decay—
fur, scurf, manure, mould, and chaff.
Perhaps you will stumble on the fleshy flooring:
the stubble of a dream waiting to be dreamt?
the husk of an unresolved echo?
No one knows:
knowing no longer matters.

Come back outside—
lift your hands and bare feet
to the eventide,
and be pierced in those good places.
Let your whole, sleeping soul
be purchased by this unleavened hour.

≈ Hardwood

Maple.
The most important hardwood in Michigan.
A stately tree with twigs smooth, pale brown,
becoming gray and smooth on the branches;
old trunks dark gray, deeply furrowed,
often cleaving on one edge in long, thick plates.
–Charles Herbert Otis

1

Wood adores the worship
of my father's hands—
whole hands,
chapped and weather-cracked,
that easily bleed.
Beneath the ointment
of his pivoting palms
angels unbraid
from within the grain,
yield song and wing
to the tongue
of his decent rhythms.

2

I never tire of trees—
their silent bark,
limbs aloft,
leaves splayed
in fanned patterns
of green on green,
roots roving deep to meet
the summoning earth.

3

Leaf's rim—
a crisp ledge,
furthest edge
of unsheathed growth,
a silhouette torn
round or flame-shaped
out of the stunning air.
Mind strains,
cannot contain,
the insouciant cycle,
balls up and bursts
like unsalted faith.

4

For there is hope of a tree
if it be cut down,
then it will sprout again,
and the tender bough thereof
will not cease. (Job 14:7)

≈ In That Moment

1st Lt. John Washington, Catholic
1st Lt. Alexander Goode, Jewish
1st Lt. George Fox, Protestant
1st Lt. Clark Poling, Protestant
have given the world an eloquent example
of toleration, charity, and the true spirit of brotherhood.
–Harry S. Truman, December 9, 1947

a boy
(too young
to be called a man)
sounds above the tumult
edges his way through throng
of hysterical soldiers
to group of chaplains:
Padre! I've lost my life jacket
and the extras are all gone
and I can't swim!
chaplain tears off life jacket
puts it around boy's shoulders:
Take this. I won't need it. I'm staying.
other three chaplains follow suit
give life jackets
to those who have none

*   *   *   *   *

In that moment,
all noises cease,
the heart is righted,
mind stills.

Word, gesture, event
are one. The hand
moves precisely, knowing
not choosing;
circumstance is not charged
with morality
or beatitude.
The animal prowl for safety
vanishes.
In that moment—
Take this. I won't need it. I'm staying.—
the pores of the body
widen and split;
we become host to deities
who flutter and spill
through our hands
as water through filtering gills;
we are borne on something more
than trust or gravity.

    *   *   *   *   *

I swim away from ship
turn to watch—
flares light up everything
bow comes up
she slides under
last thing I see:
chaplains up there
praying for safety of men—
I did not see them again

600 men lost
less than 300 survivors

Purple Heart
Distinguished Service Cross
awarded posthumously
to four chaplains
citation reads:
3 February 1943
en route to Greenland
troop transport U.S.A.T. Dorchester
torpedoed in North Atlantic
begins to plunge rapidly
confusion, darkness
men helpless through fear
chaplains move about deck
encouraging
assisting men
after supply of life jackets exhausted
they give up their own
remain aboard ship
go down with it
offering words and prayers
to the last

*   *   *   *   *

In that moment,
there is no God,
no heaven or earth,
only a steady prayer
that settles us deeper
within rising water
...*Sh'ma Yisra'el, Adonai Eloheinu, Adonai Ekhad*...
hands over hands
reach for ours,
clasp,

then release
…forgive us our trespasses, as we forgive
those who trespass against us…
our life is for being here,
and then we are gone
…Sancta Maria, Mater Dei, ora pro nobis
peccatoribus, nunc et in hora mortis nostrae….

∾ Mother Ann's Children

If I owned the whole world,
I would turn it all into joyousness.

–Mother Ann Lee

They dance in grand designs
of psalm-sweeps and spirit-flails,
damp hair springing from foreheads,
ready to scent the Master's feet
or Mother's hands with sweated joy.
They are the winged drunk,
arms lust-wide to gather and hold
their inherited portion.

Each face is gospel pith,
robbed of all but the burning wick
of emptiness.
Quickened, inwrought, flaming faces,
turning and turning—
each a mother, each a father,
each a mirror reflecting All.

≈ The Road You Seek

"In the midst of the world," the creator said to Adam,
"I have placed thee, so though couldst look around thee
as a being neither celestial nor earthly, neither mortal
nor immortal alone, so that thou shouldst
be thy own free moulder and overcomer..."
–Pica della Mirandola

The road you seek has no true lay
Of measured trope or circuitry
And deigns no boon of reveille,
Nor courts a brash audacity.

What lies without begins within,
The mobius connects at whim,
Incautious as the dealer's spin,
Empty of choice and karmic sin.

The foot must fall in treasured pools
Of cherished doubts and shadow truths.
Unremedied and truest fools
Are best prepared for Zero Rule.

No roof, however sloped or wide,
Has ever cursed or codified
Sufficiently the *termini*
Whose commonwealth is deicide.

≈ Alone

8:00 am;
two men,
twice my age
or more,
talking:

"It was hard,
sitting in that room,
watching my father
lying there, dying.
Here was a man,
who was really a man,
cryin' in his sleep
because he hurt so much."

Barber says:
"Shave around your ears?"

Man in the chair nods, says:
"You would've liked my father.
Trapped in Siberia
for months during the war.
Used to shoot pheasants offa horses
to keep his aim up."

Barber nods, says:
"Fall's in the air.
Makes the blankets feel good
around you."

≈ A High Place:
Edenville United Methodist Church, 1883 – 1983

The purpose of this pamphlet
is to put together some of the happenings
of "The Little White Church on the Hill."
  –THE WOMEN'S SOCIETY OF CHRISTIAN SERVICE

June 6, 1883:
cornerstone laid

January 18, 1884:
Gladwin County Record:
M.E. Church in Edenville completed—
$1,700.00—
dedicated Sunday—
Reverends A.J. Sprague
A.H. Younglove presiding—
debt of $700.00 remains—
pledges of $835.00
on 100 days' time secured—
a credit to Edenville
and to Mr. Younglove
faithful pastor

1900:
purchase of organ a matter of controversy
Not fitting for a house of God!
somebody yells
Psalm 149! somebody else yells
Praise in dance...sing praise
with timbrel and harp!
Ida Harper is first organist—

Olive Flock, Daisy Glover, William Secor,
Charles Hunter, Minnie Harper, Charles Harper
meet Friday nights for choir practice
Hope, Averill, Edenville
on same circuit—
one minister in charge—
Edenville's worship service
in the evenings—
when weather is bad
and bad roads worse
minister spends night
with some good family
with a spare room—
pastor is partly paid
with canned fruit and vegetables

1903 - 1905:
weight of belfry
spreads church walls—
during pastorate of J.M.P. Jarrett
church remodeled—
belfry put on its own foundations
stained glass windows installed
at $25.00 each
annex added—
project is financed by box socials
ice cream socials
home talent entertainments
church suppers (25 cents a plate)

Anna Bacon
crawls through a hole in wall
down to furnace (one lunger)

to build a fire—
one time
she is frightened
when she surprises
a sleeping stranger
come in out of the cold—
Mrs. Bacon never volunteers
to build Sabbath fire again

1923:
church closes
supporters have moved away
young people have left
to find employment

1929:
women readying the church
for a funeral
discuss the sad state of affairs
especially children not getting
any religious education—
Ladies Aid organized
pledges to commence
a Sunday School
which meets the following Easter—
Charles Hahn assigned to Edenville Church

1939:
Methodist Episcopal Church
Methodist Episcopal Church South
Methodist Protestant Church
all merge under the name
Methodist Church

through efforts
of Women's Society of Christian Service
church is painted and re-shingled
electric lights installed
chancel carpeted
choir is re-organized and robed
ceiling in sanctuary is lowered
curtains replace sagging doors to annex
new hymnals are purchased
basement is rebuilt
to serve as kitchen and dining room

Methodist Men
meet every second Sunday
for breakfast
at a close or local restaurant
sponsor one dinner a year
to raise working funds—
during an oyster stew supper
Charley Smith
mistakenly pours some stew
into his coffee
and accuses the cooks
of using river water
to make the coffee—
they didn't
but talk of digging
for good water starts—
church board is prodded
into action when a cracked board
pinches and holds fast
a lady visitor
in outside toilet—

good wells are hard to get
on top of a hill—
Run a line down the hill
and under the river
to a flowing well
on the Wixom estate.
Lawrence Davids says
Put the well
on church property.
Have faith
it will be good water.
I'll stand all costs.
water on church site
is sweetest in Edenville

1969:
thieves steal organ
microphones
amplifiers
speakers
seven of eight lower portions
of stained glass windows

1983:
people are still the same
but older
but so is the church—
membership today of 60
Sunday School attendance
between 25 and 30—
we will not attend
the next centennial
but with faith
the church will

Mildred Bell Smith:
When we cross the river and go east up the hill,
We arrive at the church of Edenville.
We pause for a moment to look at the view
And are thankful for those who long ago knew
That although we may worship our Lord anywhere,
A high place is special; we're glad to be there.

≈ Cuttings from a Witness

To be a witness does not consist in engaging in propaganda
or even in stirring people up, but in being a living mystery;
it means to live in such a way that one's life would not make sense if God
did not exist.

–Dorothy Day
(paraphrasing the Archbishop of Paris)

stop seeking divinity—
appreciate
your own eyesight
the sounds
of your feet
on stony paths
your voice lifted
in vulgar psalms:
eventually
(or perhaps not at all)
that which you seek
will begin its ascent
to you

*   *   *   *   *

in my uncertainty
is
my salvation

*   *   *   *   *

when poetry matters
paradise
will commence

*   *   *   *   *

hills the shape
of clouds

clouds the shape
of hills—
neither resents
the other's imitation

*　　*　　*　　*　　*

when time
is not a distraction
but another comfortable home—
when others
are not interruptions
but eagerness enfleshed—
when trust
is breathed like air
(and as easily forgotten
so certain am I of it)—
when joy
is the crook in the neck
where my head rests—
when my heart starts beating
without anxiety—
when I am not frightened
of being forgotten:
I can die

*　　*　　*　　*　　*

truest life
is lived
somewhere
between solitude
and surrender

*　　*　　*　　*　　*

death
is not a mystery
only

a reminder
of our familiar fruition

*   *   *   *   *

I believe
in the imagination
more than fact
though one
can lead to the other—
I believe
in art
more than religion
though both depend
on mystery—
I believe
in poetry
more than technology
though both only need
a stick
and some sand—
I believe
in silence
more than song
though each requires
the other

*   *   *   *   *

gossip
is nothing but the truth
wanting free

*   *   *   *   *

when Augustine of Hippo
held a water-rounded stone
he thought of music first
then of God

≋ Deadhead

–a found poem by Dr. Joseph Sherk, 1883-1959

I met conditions as they were—
appendectomies by kerosene lamplight;
deliveries with no assistance
(once: interlocking heads of twins—
a double-headed monster);
tracheotomies done by filing the end
off a metal male catheter, boiling it,
running heavy linen thread through it,
knotting it, inserting it into the trachea,
then tying it and anchoring it
around the patient's neck;
designing and welding splints
from 1/4-inch-round iron
at the lumber camp forge;
riding freights and logging trains;
snowshoeing alone
eight to ten miles a night with my bag;
driving a team of horses 50 miles in one day
with the thermometer at 25 below;
driving the ice 28 miles
from Cedarville to St. Ignace
with the stars as my guides
and ropes with slipknots
around the horses' necks
leading back to the sleigh,
so if the team fell through,
I could choke them
and roll them out;
attending clean and respectable poverty,
filthy and degraded poverty,
sinful and saintly poverty;

witnessing the entire band
of human intelligence
and human emotions;
driving the hours alone
and realizing:
life is selfish, possessive, creative.

The laws of the jungle
are the laws of nature,
are the laws that govern us.
We observe and radiate
the products of forces
doing their functions,
unseen and unsung.
Self-interest dominates.
Reason is something we apply
to others and everything outside ourselves—
reason controls when the sea is smooth,
but emotions control us in the storm.

One night, I was called upline
to a woodsman's tar-paper shack
that had burned down.
I hopped the first freight and jumped off
half an hour later and went in about a mile.
The fire had burned out. Dawn was breaking.
The air was still. I was alone.
I walked to the sight of the fire
through large snow-flowers gliding down,
piling on the naked limbs of birches,
weighting the branches of cathedral-spired spruces,
covering everything
except five dark mounds,
which, only hours before,
had been five, carefree children.

The scene *held* me.
My eyes blurred.
The shrill cry of a whistle
pierced the stillness.
The scene *held* my blurred eyes.
I turned my back in the eerie light
and hurried to the track
and flagged a black monster down
and tried to forget.

I've never cared to be the key log in a jam
or to crash fast over rapids—
I enjoy being a deadhead,
a partially-floating log
in my own, eddying stream,
frozen in winter and forced downstream
by ice and high water
from thawing snow in spring,
dried out in summer sun
and moved again a little by fall freshets.
When the sun sets,
leave your day
(its errors, successes, pleasures, heartaches)
with it.
If your passing be not
a Lake Superior summer sunset,
but only the faint glow
of a decaying deadhead,
at least feel that you have contributed something
to the life of the unknown stream
in which you have been thrown.
Face the east.
Profit by the day gone before.
Begin.

≈ Where God Learns

I don't think anyone could get real deep inside me.
I may sound selfish, but I want to keep a little spot
inside myself, just for me. A spot that even I
don't understand.

–Harold Allen Moe

To the few who can hear,
listen radically to me:
love.
Love—*behold,*
anyone who refuses to call you
by your true name;
love—*receive,*
those who mutilate
your reputation;
love—*cherish,*
those who use words
that wound;
love—*bless,*
the company of the cold-hearted.

Quietly turn away
from anyone who corrupts you;
do not attempt to retrieve anything
that has been taken from you.

Give your talents
to the world
that craves them,
with no strings attached;
be gentle with those

who take advantage of you
as you quietly leave them
to their own conceits.

Love in others
what you love in yourself,
tolerate in others
what you find intolerant
in yourself;
see others in your "I,"
your "I" in others.

How are you perfected
by loving the loveable?
The cock-smitten
and swelled-headed
do likewise.

Does returning kindness for kindness
nurture virtue?
The bone-idle,
the gluttonous,
the continually indignant
can do as much.

Is Lady Wisdom exalted
when you give-to
to get-back?
Any of the green-eyed
and greedy
has this art refined.

So, my little flock:
be fiercely
and indiscriminately
open-hearted;
be salt/star/stone/root/
water/wine/rose/light—
and you shall incarnate
absolutely.

≈ A-gatewards

for Chad Timothy Hoover

...when a man discovers his heart, he is properly a person.
–Hierotheos of Nafpotkos

This time, I can only go as far
as the gate with you.
Lift the latch now,
and turn up your palms,
and I will kiss them,
and then you must go,
walk (finally alone)
into places of forest and frost.
Don't look back, it's no use:
home will never be
where it once was.

You must go
where education and religion assassinate,
where mysticism is reduced to chemistry,
lamentation to pathology,
compassion to naiveté,
justice to winning.
You must make
homes of others' houses,
pets of others' animals,
love in others' languages;
sing to saints never born,
sift through corpses of holy writ,
sigh to gods always in distress,
mistake success for fulfillment,
integrity for faithfulness,
death for failure.

You will find the woman
who has lain so long on her kitchen floor
that her cheekskin has fused with the wood
and the man beneath the bathwater
who was scalded when his heart arrested
as he was turning on the tap.

One afternoon, walking home from the career
that has never spelled your name correctly,
a hard winter rain will fall and fall
and saturate your thick, brown coat
and your fur cap,
and you will be re-begotten—
by the light in the water
around you,
within you,
and the light on the pathless path
where you've turned.
From now on:
you will never be lost,
for being found
is no longer your vocation;
you will never be blind,
for your vision
does not require sight;
you will never be deaf,
for your ears have roots
in the unsayable;
you will never be frightened,
for true suffering has become
your doxology;
you will never again taste desire,
for you have become the brother of joy.

⌇ Emblem

...the old rugged cross...has a wondrous attraction for me.
–Reverend George Bennard

back buttocks legs
are scourged
with flagellum

lacerations
tear into skeletal muscles
produce orthostatic hypotension
and hypovolemic shock

victim is thrown
to ground
on back
in preparation
for transfixion
of hands

scourged wounds
become contaminated
with dirt

each respiration scrapes
stripped skin
against wood of stipes

wrists are nailed
to patibulum
with 7-inch iron spikes

driven
through flexor retinaculum
and intercarpal ligaments
severing sensorimotor median nerve

ischemic contractures
and impalement of ligaments
produce clawlike grasp

patibulum
is lifted
onto stipes

sedulum
in center of stipes
supports victim
knees
are bent
and rotated laterally

feet are fixed
to front
of stipes
by iron spike
driven
through second
intermetatarsal space
and distal tarsometatarssal joint
distressing peroneal nerve
and branches
of medial and lateral
plantar nerves

weight of body
pulling down
on outstretched
(not taut)
arms and shoulders
fixes intercostal muscles
in an inhalation state

lungs begin to collapse
in small areas

hypoxia and hypercarbia
soon result

onset of tetanic contractions
further hinders respiration

lack of compensation
by kidneys
due to loss of blood
from scourging
increases strain
on heart
which beats faster

fluid builds up
in lungs

friable non-infective thrombotic vegetations
form on aortic valve
dislodge and embolize
into coronary circulation
producing acute
transmural myocardial infarction

⇜ Part Two ⇝

≈ The Diary of a Call and a Coming-to

...and a man shall not come to save his own soul.
Let his soul go to hell.
He shall come because he knows that his own soul
is not the be-all and end-all,
but that all souls of all things do but compose
the body of God, and that God indeed shall BE.
–D. H.Lawrence (in a letter to Juliette Huxley)

Friday, 9:00 PM. Sitting in my underwear in Room 203 in the guest-house at the Abbey of Our Lady of Gethsemani. The air conditioner was blowing hard when I came in, but I turned if off and opened the windows partway to let in real air—heat-scented, windless, and brimming with night babble. Poked my head into the twilight-lit sanctuary as I came up the stairs. Thought I saw two birds, but the wingsounds were quieter than feather and bone in flight: bats. Arrived toward evening, put my few things away, and went back outside and sat beneath the limbs of a sheltering gingko near a wall of the enclosure until Vespers.

Vespers: monk voices lobbing psalms against high, white walls that vault them evermore upward until the words become sounds and the sounds ensheathe one another in a forming and re-forming echo that lazily ricochets inside my skull.

I am all alone, anonymous here, unacknowledged by nothing other than slight nods or sometimes a smile or a soft hello in one of the corridors. I am not here for society. I am here to meet myself outside the human cords that bind me to others in various and usual ways. The meeting is difficult and is as essential as it is absurd—following a blind hunger that bawls to be tended. So I bring it for succor and suckling, to this many-breasted region. God is no more nor less in this place than in the action of my bending over and tying my shoelace, but this place is apart. Responsibilities are lifted, and I am cared for. The desert becomes more silent and a special loneliness more keenly felt. Time is measured in cycles and in subtle turnings. Words have no primacy here, nor do names or the casual trappings of identity; lack of speech, not eloquence, is a charism. Here, the rope slaps the flagpole, a field is in profound *gestus,* a glass holds milk or water as they are—free. Free in the way that anything is free when it reserves nothing of itself. Here, we are men wombed by other men, responding to the Unbegun from within a darkened seed of silence.

I want to soften, wind down, not push—retreat to the place that is dark within and feared—my own heart: the place that I protect that is most me and, for some reasons, most unacceptable to me. I want to move lower, into the darker light of darkness where God resides more thickly. God cannot be sought. This I know: the very seeking after God creates a barrier, as though what I seek is separate from me. When I breathe and am aware of my breathing, I "find" God. In the urge that brought me to this place, among these men in their deep-dark brown and cream garb, I "find" God. In seeing the sun-heated, cloister walls surrounding me, God is "found." Certain faces intrigue me with their intensity or beauty or blankness, and I want to snoop and penetrate demeanor with questions, but I have my own, growing stillness to honor, and already, thoughts are leaping and slashing less, are less seductive, and I am more able to give them up to their vaudevillian ways.

*   *   *   *   *

Found two pinecones on the hillside next to the cemetery next to the garden and brought them back to 203 and jammed a white candle and a stick of incense in them. The room smells sweet and woody.

Thomas Merton in **Conjectures of a Guilty Bystander:** *God passes. God remains. We pass. In and out. God passes. We remain. We are nothing. We are everything. God is in us. God is gone from us. God is not there. We are here in God.*

*   *   *   *   *

Memory: Uncle Leo, one of my mother's nine brothers, lives with us for a couple of summers in a row in the late '50's. One night, I hear him stumble into my bedroom (he always slept with me) drunk and giggle to himself as he urinates out the windowscreen. He crawls into bed with me, and spends the next half hour teaching me the Lord's Prayer. Now, everytime I hear it or say it, the smell of malt and hops is twined around every syllable of that merciful poem.

*   *   *   *   *

Saturday. Dream last night: I am with a young man and woman. The three of us are walking down a flight of stairs to a cellar.
The young man is God. God has lain his arms across our necks, the young woman's and mine. He asks us to show him some things about life. This strikes me as very odd. I say, "No! You!" and I start to pull myself out from under his arm. God yanks me to himself, but I am not restrained by his harsh grip. Even though he has me clutched closely to him, I jerk away and move up the stairs from him. As I look at the young-man God, deep lines begin to crease his darkening face, and the skin beneath his eyes is blackening. I can no longer look into God's face. This is not God. I wake up, frightened.

*   *   *   *   *

Woke in time for Lauds at 5:45 and walked into the church barefoot-ed (every Eden deserves such praise!). Treacly dawnlight sloping through slender windows; psalms sung in a desultory drone in the moist, unmoving air. Only four of us in the pews; one, a woman. A bird had flown in and was frantic to escape. I'd hoped it would let loose with a trill of panic—in that arcature of stone, glass, and seething sacrament, such sound would translate as praise. It didn't. What are we doing on this day, at this moment in our lives, in this place? What is this place? Who are they? Me?

I *heard* the gospel tale as it was being read from Saint Luke's book: *Jesus was at table with the two men. He took their warm bread, blessed it, broke it, and passed it, broken, to them. At once, they saw him, and as they did, he vanished. They turned, stunned, to one another. One said, "Didn't our hearts yearn and glow while he spoke to us on the road, explaining the old stories?"*

They hurried to Jerusalem, to the remnant of disciples and their friends, and said to them, "Jesus is back among us!" And as they tried to speak of their experience on the road to Emmaus that led to their recognition of Jesus the moment he split the bread, Jesus was suddenly among them.

The word *broken* reared up for me, and this question: how did these two know where to find the followers who'd hidden themselves so as not to be discovered by anyone who might associate them with the lunacy of love that Jesus roused and was?

*   *   *   *   *

Pinned to the bulletin board downstairs is this neatly-typed note: "Important: A bull is running with our cow herd in the pasture on the opposite side of the highway, so it is inadvisable to walk through the area."

*   *   *   *   *

I've brought a mug with me that was once my grandparent's. A piece from the set of dishes they bought from Sears and Roebuck as a tenth anniversary gift for themselves. Virginia Rose, the pattern is called. Rinsed it out in the bathroom sink with the miniature bar of Ivory soap. Slick lather on hands. Fingers sliding against bone-colored glass. How many gallons and gallons of coffee has it held? How many mouths—and whose?—have curled lips over rim to sip and gulp? Heft of it in my left hand as blue towel wipes inside and outside dry. Remembering that the washing and drying of an 80-year-old coffee mug can be an act as unerring as the birth of an epoch.

*　　　*　　　*　　　*　　　*

Water that has formed on the leaves during the night fall onto a path as I half-walk, half-skid down it to the valley floor. The sound is of rough silk being carefully folded by chapped hands. I stop to listen better. The dripping and the birds' breakfast songs seem to come from a place of silence that is as quiet as the sunlight falling in precise angles through the mist I am entering. For a moment, I am not listening at all: I am part of a sound that is hearing itself through me in utter stillness. Then, a crackle and a *woosshh*. A white-tailed deer leaps past me, so close I can smell the funk of its fur. Such appalling beauty. The speed, the grace, the size. All I can do is stand—an electric tremor slicing and reverberating through my body-drenched in appreciation of this moment: the unending presentation of growth and rot, merging, surging, toward, and within, one another; the rump of the deer bounding through a clump of elder trees whose sides are plashed in golden light. All I can do is breathe and see, my eyes ordering all these elements into splendor.

The asphalt path nose-diving to the valley bottom is about as wide as a Buick Roadster and bordered on either side by a baroque, airy tangle of bittersweet, feverfew, wild mint, goldenrod, and collar-high bushes that have no name to me. A fine web of coursing vines—fragile-seeming but bred to conquer—binds the over- and undergrowth together. Four rods south from where the path suddenly ends, rises—or, more precisely, presides—the seven-storey focus of this green court—a sycamore tree more than a century old. From a distance, her bark looks like water-damaged muslin; up-close, it is, as Colonial settlers used to say, more like scraped-off wallpaper. Limbs enough for a month of fires lie akimbo in a radius around her base. Hollow limbs, much lighter than their spied bulk suggests, limbs curled in the stylized contour of a geisha.

The sun, it's obvious, is humming one of the epistle sonatas to himself, else why this Mozartian light—gin-clear and cocksure, exuberantly pressing its golden flare against the leaves' backsides, rousing them to luminescence? Why these bassoon shadows flinging muscular alleluias across the valley and halfway up its western slope? Someone has mown the floor, and the entire swale billows with a brew of vegetal huskiness. I stand in the middle of this blatant *sanctus,* peeing; aiming myself with one hand and balancing two books, my mugful of coffee in the other. A pencil, a pen, and a legal pad are tucked under my chin.

Birds are now loud in the air, in the trees—winged sound, sung song, the air brimful of peeps, twitterings, and flute-like gurglings. The Great Comfort is in their throats, the cosmic in the homely. Invisible life being lived out within inches of my eyes. How I worship this coming season of fruiting, its odors and visual opiates; the way the light breaks with a clarity that shimmers without obstructing; the way it adds, in fact, detail to whatever it surrounds and penetrates. Light that is revelation as well as preparation. For endings. Why do we insist on the efficacy of permanence when all around us, and within our own cells, all is turning toward change, waning, lessening?

*   *   *   *   *

Walked the woods path to the statues of the sleeping James, John, and Peter, while a little further upslope, Jesus is in his great agony. I came upon this second statue, surprised by the posture of Jesus—upright on his knees, head flung back, head, arched, hands over his eyes, elbows V-ed to the sky. A startlement in the midst of the serene, pitch-scented grove, and a contrast to the disciples' sensual repose. I looked on the simple lines of the sculpture, at the outline of the heaving torso beneath the drape of robe, at the thrown-back head. One person stripped to a moment of consummate surrender—the freedom of one inebriated with obedience; an unglamorous *fiat* drawing the source of creation into the affairs of the exiled human spirit.

*   *   *   *   *

Rendered Paul's letter to the folks at Corinth in my own words, to meet him, here and there, in the Word:

Love is tender, supple, and intelligent.
Love does not compete nor does it easily heat
into the stiffness of anger.
Love is defenseless,
and it does not blindly serve the ceaseless desires
of the mind.
Neither is love fueled by attention,
but radiates from that which is ordinary.
Love does not say
Right or Wrong,
Masculine or Feminine,
For or Against.
Love welcomes all things,
and its understanding, care, and delight
are complete and inexhaustible.
Love never began.
Love will never end.

Shame is rigid, sober, and impatient.
Shame has all the answers, and swiftly heats
into the paralysis of perfectionism.
Shame separates,
and it serves the anxious whims of success.

Also, shame is fueled by fame
and radiates from that which is novel and dramatic.
Shame says:
Winner, Loser,
Sinner, Saint,
Members Only.
Shame welcomes only that which keeps alive
the illusion of control,
and its cleverness, promiscuity, and contempt
are complete and inexhaustible.
Shame must end.

*　　*　　*　　*　　*

Day's ebb. Long shawls of shadows unrolling over the shoulders of the knobs, and it's just plain hot. I'm back from Compline, back from supper, and back from picture-taking: a rusted length of barbed wire snaking around a knotty, unpainted post, a brown rabbit that let me sidle fairly near before loping off, stalks of wheat sprouting wild in the fissures of a brick about eight feet up the side of a wall, a sideless wagon that, from a distance, looked like an abandoned altar. Such details calm and cure, their easily-missed intimacies open out to something vast, but infinitely near—like classic haiku—and I am quick-carried to the freshets of my onrushing heart.

Midway down the path bordered by shoulder-high, black-eyed Susans, I paused and let blow through me the delirious birdsong, while the church bells' pedal-point pressed shadows into invisible tremolos of the settling sun's heat. A charm of finches scattered from overhead branches, sweeping and reeling like leaves with a purpose. Besot by such generosity, I come to: True Identity (called Christ, called Atman, called Buddha, or any one of these—Wine, Breath, Friend, Silence) is the gradual realization that I don't—and can't possibly—know who I really am. What woos me is the Eternal Pulse that rings—primally, rhythmically, sensually—within each moment, completely rooted in, while knowing Itself beyond, my body. Another way of saying the same thing: conversion is the ever-deepening awareness of the question that is my own name. I am home here. I am sure of that because I have no need of an identity. And if one appears—which happens when I'm frightened and feeling unsafe or shy—it clearly is no match for the rain against my face or the sight of a rabbit bounding into brush. When I am indentity-less, I can be lost, I can lose; I can be new and unknown to myself.

*   *   *   *   *

Czeslaw Milosz: ...a choice made now, today, projects itself backwards and changes our past.

*   *   *   *   *

Sitting on the porch outside the library, the air foaming with the locusts' electric trill, I have a kick galvanic (that had probably started earlier when I was walking among the tombstones—comforted by their grime and moss, the carved names no longer relevant to the remains underfoot—and held a handful of grass clippings to my nose and inhaled): something from long ago—a word, a book, a face—has brought me here. Something blowing back when, caught in me. Rooted, budded, blossomed, is blossoming still. And, with that, I want to weep. For all of us. For our precious, cockamamie fragility. For the unnameable fear that grabs us by the nape and shakes and shakes us. But I don't. Or can't: the tears we are born with are the heaviest and, perhaps, can never be fully wept.

*   *   *   *   *

Memory: summer of 1958. I am 10 and walking deep in the woods behind Clarence Brown's farm. I step into a clearing and stand there at its edge. I am suddenly aware of something invisible facing me, a presence charged with a great and good energy. I walk toward it, compelled. Trusting, trusting. The air, the light, the heat, the leaves, the bark of the trees all around me seeming not to be what they are, but things that leap and twirl and fuse with one another in a splendid, zany undulation. And I'm walking toward whatever it is that is that is also walking, invisibly, toward me—though it seems to be all around me, too, within the light and bark and leaves. I walk and it walks until "we" blend in a single moment of breath.

*   *   *   *   *

Sunday morning. Dream during last night's sleep, when the air had cooled to a wondrous balm. I am in a rambling, old house that has been converted into a department store. Looking through a display case at a collection of talcum powder tins, I see the initials *T.M.* in Oriental calligraphy on a 5-inch round one. I look closer. Written on a small card beside it is an explanation that the scent was inspired by the life of Thomas Merton. When I ask a saleswoman about this, she tells me that this is a way to help people recall that Merton was once among us, and it is also a memorial to the way he died.

The grass on Thomas Merton's grave is sparse, not at all of a thickness a 30-some-year-old plot ought to be sprouting. Merton beneath—where roots and rootshoots form whole, silent cities with lifeforms that rove, blind and sure, and join with the flesh of the planted dead in renewing this place from which we spring: reverdure.

*   *   *   *   *

A great whale of a day, and I am sitting smack dab in the middle of its belly—this valley again—breathing the unglossed air. A leaf, green and soft as the belly of a pup, drops onto the rotting picnic table where I've been sitting. Thoughtlessly, I put it into my mouth. I want to taste green, taste something as real and sentient as I feel. I work it over with my tongue and reach for Mark Van Doren's book, **That Shining Place,** to find a poem that will match this action. I do: "Merton's Woods":

The monastery bells can still be heard there.
Or can they? I don't know. I went down once.
By the winding path, and all I listen to was trees:
Not huge, but many and high, and busy
With birds; and the top leaves
twinkled in the sun, as did his eyes when he said at
last,
"Here is my cell." But it was a house,
New-built: a small one, with a porch.
And I listened to the trees, incessant, sacred:
More than I could count. And acorns dropped,
And squirrels scampered. Foxes, too,
He told me, played some days in the distance,
Wary of man—even of him—yet they did caper,
Lighter of foot than cats.
I must have heard the bells, but more as air, as
spicy wood,
Than bronze; as sun, as shade; as silence;
As contemplation, searching an unknown tongue.

I chew the leaf slowly without swallowing and finally spit it out onto the hairs of some nettles growing near the table.

    *   *   *   *   *

The holy emerges whenever my eyes stop seeing through the I's lens of its own extraordinariness. I cannot truly see unless I am detached from the desire to know and cling and retain. The moment I know what something should be, the form it should take, all possibility of discovery ceases. A predicted future is a premature fossil.

    *   *   *   *   *

Lunch done (the diningroom is aflood with new retreatants), I fixed myself a cup of scorched coffee and came out here to read, but I only sit, appeased by the great-hearted litany of movement. Swaying, summer-ladened limbs, small birds aflight, the flash and glide of fish in the pool, the monks' unurgent pace, a bonny breeze jazzing my arms and clean hair. I smell the cloth of my pants, too—sour with a weekend's worth of sweat and dirt and dew. I am reluctant to leave, having been suspended in a seamless, silent, furling, and unfurling medicine. The sun is fully out and shining now, and the birds are having heaven in their throats.

Today won't be as sultry as the past few. During Mass, the two bats soared through the sanctuary (theirs must be a special novitiate). The lines for confession are long. The doors here are never locked, and the world moves through them, and the monks are here—steady, put, ballast. We who come, pass through these buildings and through these monks soundlessly. Like the bats.

*   *   *   *   *

Should have climbed to the top of the hill across from the monastery driveway sooner. The view! Fields furrowed like Zen gardens. Hills vaguely resembling mosques through the scrim of heat. Air aflame with the spice of earth's cycle. Three crows circled in the east beneath a skyscape of truest blue, one cawing to the other two. Across Highway 247, the cow herd—with the bull among them, black and generously genitaled—was hoofing down toward the edge of the narrow blacktop.

This place exudes a geometry of timelessness. I walk among the well-tended dead as nonchalantly as I wander among the living, who carry books or nothing or coffee in one of the white cups from the rack in the kitchen. The bricks of the buildings, shabbied by the years, beckon with a welcome that's as fresh as their mortar once was. Fresher.

For a moment, sitting on the bench beneath the statue of Saint

Joseph pedestaled high amidst wild wheat and flowering yucca, I am unrelated to anyone, unattached—not sadly so, but in actual fact. Then comes the familiar rondeau of thought: how is it that I am sitting on a hillside next to a Trappist monastery in Kentucky as the sun drowns in its own water of fabulous color and a cow lows on the 28th day of a summer month over a hundred years after the birth of my grandmother? What is it that I follow to these hills, that calls to me without word or gesture?

Beneath what I am seeking, far beneath the words I have read and written and the few I have spoken, and beneath the listening and the silence, is a spiritual tinder that is responsible for my ignition. I have place in creation, as surely as do the stinging bugs, the humidity that cloaks me, the woods' wild perfume. Alone, I have place. With others, I have place. And, proceeding from this place, I continue to be created, though clearly, I—at some certain level—am already wholly formed. Wonderfully, invisibly, unexplainably so. The Ineffable is resident in every step, breath, and mouthful of food I've taken. There is no existence apart from that. None.

This *is* existence.

*   *   *   *   *

From this day forward, I declare myself to be totally useless—now to get down to the business of laughing!